T0149204

Everything You Need To Know
Digital Detox
© Aspen Books, 2018

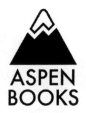

**ASPEN
BOOKS**

All rights reserved.

First published in 2018.

A catalogue record for this book is available from
the British Library.

ISBN: 978-1-9997489-4-4

Published by Aspen Books, an imprint of
Pillar Box Red Publishing Ltd.

Everything You Need To Know

DIGITAL DETOX

Log Off & Log On to Life

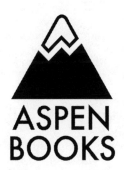

ASPEN
BOOKS

Naomi Berry

Contents

INTRO
DUCTION

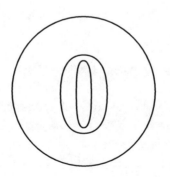

Introduction

'We shape our tools, and thereafter they shape us.' [1] - John Culkin

How many screens are in your home? Our minds immediately go to the living room and its television centerpiece, and perhaps the smaller iteration in the kitchen or bedroom. But I'm not just asking about televisions, I mean all of the screens: smartphones, computers, laptops, tablets. It's likely a much higher number than you had expected. From various reports around the world, the average home has anywhere between 7 to 10 internet-enabled devices, and more often than not, people are using a number of those screens at the same time.

Whilst screens have always been a part of the home since the dawn of the television in the 1920s, the leap from 1-2 to 7-10 is a more recent phenomenon. It is symptomatic of a societal shift that has been accelerated by the rapid evolution of smaller devices like smartphones and tablets. It gains momentum with every new development as technology forays into new territories, with watches, virtual reality game consoles and even glasses becoming increasingly digital.

The purpose of technology has also seen a significant shift from its initial premise. Devices are no longer primarily for entertainment but now for function. Technology has changed the fundamental way we approach things like writing, communicating or even something as trivial as looking for a new pair of shoes. We have even rendered entire careers extinct thanks to technological development, and we are in the process of phasing out more.

Devices are gradually coming to be more and more essential in our execution of daily actions. Morning coffees are paid for with contactless payment, clothes are ordered online, communication is made via messenger, and apps are being used to order dinner. We live in a world where technology is swiftly becoming an extension of our very being. Our relationship with digital devices is constantly developing into dependence at a rate that shows no sign of slowing down.

A Wake Up Call

Living in Seoul, one of the tech capitals of the world, means that digital devices are undeniably intrinsic to my day-to-day life.

I wake up to the sound of my phone - in turning off the alarm, I see a quick glimpse of the notifications I missed whilst asleep. I get ready, head to the station, earphones firmly in place. On the train, I am one of countless people with their heads bowed, catching up with notifications and messages, scrolling through some feeds and watching the odd random video before I arrive at the office.

Working in gaming means that I spend a borderline intimate amount of time with a great number of screens of varying sizes. I sit in front of two monitors peppered with numerous windows and tabs, with my phone running a test model or streaming eSports between them. This is my set-up for around eight hours, which, in retrospect, is probably more time than I have spent in someone's company uninterrupted. Harrowing.

But the day goes on, and I shut down my computer and clock out with my phone firmly in hand. When I get home, I turn on the television and open my laptop to drift between work, social media and mindless browsing until it is late enough for me to set the alarm on my mobile and start again.

One morning, I opted to leave my phone by my bedside. This one, spontaneous off-hand decision had an alarming, Matrix red-pill style effect that truly opened my eyes to the peculiarity of our societal 'norm'. I was suddenly hyper-aware of everyone around me on my morning commute. Despite looking around the whole time, I didn't catch a single person's eye. Everyone sat in neat rows, heads down, thumbs tapping, completely absorbed in their devices. People rose, left, entered, took seats and bumped into each other seemingly without the need of sight. The train was full, but almost completely silent. It was very bizarre to observe a mass behavior I was usually - unconsciously - a part of. Despite being a foreigner in a largely homogenous society, I had never felt more of an 'other' than I did in that train car without my iPhone.

And whilst this behavior may be somewhat of a norm, it is by no means sustainable. Overuse of technology is taking its toll on us both physically and mentally, but it is quickly disregarded as just a regular symptom of every day life. Putting in overtime, working from home, answering emails out of the office; they are all perceived as 'working hard' or being 'dedicated'. Spending time curating an aesthetically attractive feed or diligently growing a base of online followers is lauded as being 'popular' or 'well-liked'. Constant connection is presented in an overwhelmingly positive frame.

But we are burning out, operating on fumes due to digital fatigue. It is easier to place blame on a much bigger societal addiction than to criticize your own decisions, but it takes individual action to trigger change. We need to decompress. Take a step back and unplug for a second. A balance needs to be struck between our digital dependency and our offline lives. Our well-being deserves to be a top priority instead of an afterthought.

Why Digital Detox?

The concept of 'digital detox' is one that has gained a lot of prominence in the last year or so, but its core purpose is still often misunderstood. For many, it immediately conjures ideas of flushing all devices down the toilet, taking a sabbatical and spending a month in some remote tropical location, waxing lyrical about how wonderful it is to find inner peace without technology whilst on a canoe in the middle of the Indian Ocean. It is seen as something impractical and incapable of coexisting with regular day-to-day life. It requires a sacrifice of not only technology, but also time, money, routine and energy.

Whilst those indulgent trips are often the most prominently featured in the Google search results for 'digital detox', they are undoubtedly the most misleading. The focus of a digital detox is not the 'event'; it is a reflection, analysis and adjustment of your own behavior in relation to the digitally driven society around you. Skyscanner is not required to start a digital detox, just a desire to develop healthier habits. By embracing a digital detox, you are making a conscious effort to improve the following:

- Your overall mood

- Daytime fatigue

- Quality of sleep

- Productivity

- Stress and anxiety

- Memory capacity

- Connections with loved ones

Hopefully this book will help you find a way to unplug and reconnect to the world around you. Technology ought to serve us, not the other way around, and we need to find the right balance between the two. This book is not about eradicating technology; it's about embracing and enhancing the other aspects of your life that may have inadvertently fallen to the wayside due to our growing dependence on devices.

It's time to log off and log on to life.

DIAGNOSIS

▷ What is Technology Addiction?

When was the last time you picked up your phone? Five minutes ago? Ten seconds ago? Is it sitting in your other hand as you read this now? NYU Professor Adam Alter found that the average millennial checks their phone 150 times a day.[1] Could you keep track of the number of times you picked up your phone on a daily basis? Or how much time you spent on it each time? Is it too daunting of a task to try to ascertain how much of your day takes place in the presence of a screen?

Technology addiction is by no means a medically classified affliction, but rather an umbrella, catch-all term used to describe our growing dependence on all things digital: the Internet, our computers, our tablets and our mobile phones. It has become a modern phenomenon that has grown its legs and gained its speed as technology has become more and more intrinsic in society, and it is beginning to outrun any means we have to stop it.

Linguistically, the word 'addiction' is something we have always used in conjunction with very negative nouns, substances like alcohol or drugs, but rarely in relation to something so common and prevalent in our day-to-day lives. Play word association with 'addiction' and our minds are more likely to jump to publicly condemned compound nouns like 'tobacco addiction' than they are likely to land on 'technology'. But technology addiction is very real. Researchers found those forced to go cold turkey from devices have displayed similar symptoms to smokers who are suffering nicotine withdrawals.[2]

We live in a world in which the line between technology being our biggest helper and biggest crutch is increasingly thinning.

And the signs of addiction are not as obvious as we are used to, either. It is not a pallid skin tone or involuntary twitch that gives a technology addict away. 'Traditional' addiction has very telling signs that stand out because they are different from the normal person's behavior; technological addiction has managed to slide under the radar because its symptoms have - somehow - become ingrained as 'regular' in today's society. Who is more likely to catch your eye on a crowded train car: the guy reading a hardcover or the bowed heads of those surrounding him, eyes glued to their phone screens?

However, all hope is not lost. It's a problem that we are becoming increasingly aware of, as Google Trends reports a steady increase over the past five years of searches for 'phone addiction' – ironically, likely searched for on phones. 'Social media addiction' is another search term that has increased in frequency. We have identified a potential problem and are searching for solutions.

Thus, the birth of the digital detox: not a method of shunning technology completely, but a means of allowing ourselves to take a step back in a world dominated by digital.

▷ The Toll of Technology

The most natural response to hearing 'digital detox' for the first time is not necessarily 'no', but rather 'how?' Technology has become so integrated in our lives that it is difficult to imagine trying to cut it down.

Sure, it's not nice to hear you spend too much time on your phone or behind your computer, but whilst you may believe you're capable of exercising moderation, there are genuine concerns for our health with the overuse of technology.

Technology and the Body

Not a single reader can say they grew up without hearing the warning that our eyes will turn square if you stare at a screen for too long. Of course, there is a little truth behind it; countless studies have shown that our eyes just aren't made to be fixed on screens. The Vision Council found 60% of American adults have experienced eyestrain from prolonged screen exposure.[1] Even still, we don't require numbers to acknowledge that the longer we sit behind our computer screens, the drier and more fatigued our eyes become.

And a bout of dryness is only one of the issues our eyes face when glued to a screen all day. Reading from screens can cause tension headaches due to the high contrast between the dark text and brightly lit backgrounds. Devices designed for longer periods of reading - such as Kindles and other electronic readers - display black text on grey backgrounds. Mobile phones and computer screens make no such allowance for our poor peepers. Square-eyed? Try bone-dry and aching... being square would be the least of their problems.

Unfortunately, as digital devices become more intrinsic to our routines, the concerns of technology use have evolved beyond metaphorically changing one's eye shape; it is now literally changing the shape of our bodies. Kenneth Hansraj, a leading New York surgeon, recently published a study that stated the 60-degree angle we tilt our heads to look at our phones is putting around an added 60 pounds of pressure on our necks, which leads to aching and misalignment. This additional strain on our necks can result in the loss of our cervical spine's natural curve, which causes a whole other plethora of problems (primarily premature deterioration) that could require surgery.[2]

It's also no new groundbreaking discovery to hear that listening to music through your headphones all day is not exactly the greatest for your aural health. An analysis by the Journal of the American Medical Association found that the reported number of teens with hearing loss today is significantly higher than those three decades ago, and it may be attributable to in-ear headphone use.[3]

Additionally, for men out there, don't forget the bonus threat to your fertility. According to a study lead by the University of Exeter, the radio-frequency electromagnetic radiation emitted from mobile devices is extremely detrimental to sperm quality.[4] In layman's terms: keeping your phone in your pocket is sniping your chance at becoming a father one day. Oh, and sitting with your laptop on well, your lap, as the name suggests, isn't advised either. The additional heat also isn't the most future-family-friendly.

And it's not just the inside of our internal body that's suffering here; take a moment to think about the amount of bacteria that calls your phone screen home. Now think about how often that phone screen is pressed up on the side of your face? Ah, yes, just the gift your skin was asking for. Hello, eczema and acne triggers.

Technology and the Mind

Our minds are no less at the mercy of our new digital age than our bodies. Who can truly say whether it is necessarily a good thing for our brains to now be able to access the world's wealth of information at any time? Were we built to be as constantly connected as we are now?

Our modern world has seen hypochondriacs evolve - akin to a Pokémon reaching its final, most powerful form - to a whole new monster so rampant that it earned ultimate recognition with an entry in the Oxford English Dictionary:

Cyberchondriac: A person who compulsively searches the Internet for information about particular real or imagined symptoms of illness. (OED)

Microsoft's spell-check may not acknowledge it (judging by the multiple angry red squiggles it elicits each time it is typed) but 'cyberchondriac' is the new peaky paranoia. When suspecting illness, hypochondriacs of the past only had their own worst thoughts before being diagnosed by the doctor; today's cyberchondriacs literally have every book and medical journal at their fingertips. Googling a simple cold sore can run all the way to bullous impetigo. If you've got a cough, you could be anywhere between a common cold and (particularly if Yahoo Answers is involved) certain death. WebMD or NHS 24 may misdiagnose your sneeze, but searching symptoms online can have a very real effect on your health by inducing anxiety.

Speaking of anxiety, it doesn't take a medical expert to tell you that social media is a huge stress trigger, but they'll certainly continue to do so anyway. A study by the Edinburgh Business School found that the more friends one has on Facebook, the more anxious they are likely to be in regards to their online behavior and how it is perceived and consequently judged.[5]

But it's not just your behaviour on social media that has a bearing on mental health, but also - and perhaps more immediately obvious - the behavior of those you are observing. We know it's not healthy to compare ourselves to others, but social media essentially invites the concept, and most worryingly, presents an edited, filtered, and biased point of comparison.

Self-esteem stumbles as technology soars. Airbrushing was once a highly protested practice exclusive to celebrities and models in glossy magazines. Now, apps with the same capabilities have become commonplace on smartphones to retouch the humble selfie. Countless studies have found links between viewing others' selfies and feeds to feelings of inadequacy. Over 60 million photos are uploaded to Instagram every day, and the vast majority show a carefully staged and considered capture; the best foot is always most calculatedly placed forward. The University of Missouri published a study that found that the repeated use of social media could lead to symptoms of depression if feelings of envy were triggered.[6]

Of course, technology is by no means some sort of vehicle engineered by Satan himself to facilitate the downfall of man. One could compile an equally scary read on the effects of dieting, reading, or even knitting (carpal tunnel; you'd be surprised). The 'evils of technology' presented in this chapter are not here to decry all that is digital or ward you off of all devices until the end of time, it's just to shine a little light on the worst-case scenarios that are becoming more prevalent in today's culture as exercising less moderation becomes a societal norm. These extremes are what a digital detox could prevent from occurring.

▷ Do You Need a Digital Detox?

So you've learnt about technology addiction and read about the tolls it can have on the body and mind. Have you managed to place yourself in this whole situation yet? Where do you fall on the spectrum of digital dependence? Do you need a digital detox?

Sometimes it's hard to look frankly at yourself and analyse your own habits, so this quiz is designed to be an easy method of assessment that doesn't require too critical of an eye on your lifestyle. Simply answer 'yes' or 'no' to the questions below. You're the only one who will ever see your responses, so don't lie to yourself; be honest with your answers before you count them up and look at the results. (Likewise, if you think someone you know relies a little too heavily on their tech, think about them in regards to these questions before you stage your grand intervention.)

The Digital Dependence Quiz

- When you wake up in the morning, do you check for messages, emails and notifications before you even hit the bathroom?

- And before you go to sleep, do you regularly use some form of digital device in bed?

- Do you check your phone when you wake up during the middle of the night?

- Have you ever used social media in real social situations, like at lunch with a friend, or at a party?

- Do you multi-screen? For example, watched TV and used your phone, used a tablet and your laptop etc.

- Have you physically fallen or bumped into someone because you were too distracted using your device?

- Do you regularly eat lunch at your desk when you don't have assignments?

- When completing a task, do you regularly take breaks to look at the same sites/apps repeatedly?

- Have you ever felt separation anxiety when you've left your phone at your desk, or at home?

- Do you take your phone to the bathroom with you?

- Have you chosen to FaceTime family or friends over real face-to-face time?

- Do you delay meals to take a photo, or rearrange the table for a more favourable shot before anyone is allowed to tuck in?

- Have you felt like your phone has rung or vibrated when it hasn't? Fun fact: this is an actual condition called Phantom Vibration Syndrome.

- Do you carry a charger or an external battery?

- Have you ever thought of captions or hashtags in advance?

- Do you make a point to record concerts purely to flex on social media, with the intention of never watching the footage back again?

- Have you sat a child down in front of a digital device in a restaurant or any other public area?

So how did you do?

<u>If you answered 'yes' 0-4 times:</u>

It's impossible for us to live our lives without technology, and you don't seem to be too dependent on your devices. You might be more interested in unplugging for a weekend than making any major lifestyle changes.

<u>If you answered 'yes' 5-9 times:</u>

Whilst there's no cause for alarm, there may be cause for reflection and adjustment. You use devices quite regularly throughout your day and likely without a second thought; it wouldn't hurt to consider cutting back a little. Try out a week's plan.

<u>If you answered 'yes' 10+ times:</u>

Are you propping this page open with your mobile, balancing the book on an open laptop and watching Netflix right now? Okay, maybe you're not at that extreme yet (yet), but it's not that far of a leap to make. You seem to be quite dependent on technology and would most definitely benefit from developing some healthier digital habits across a 30-day period.

HOW TO START

▷ 9 Commandments

Before you embark on any lifestyle-changing process, it's a good idea to have a solid set of rules... Perhaps not 'rules', per se, but rather tenets, that you should keep in mind to abide and draw from. It's a staple: yoga has its doctrine; paleo has its principles, and the digital detox has these - the Nine Commandments. Each of the commandments will be expanded upon in different sections of the book, but think of this like a little summarised go-to cheat sheet to make the most out of your digital detox.

① *Pace Yourself*

When you're starting a digital detox, it's key to remember that going cold turkey is never the answer. Unless you're one of those cardiganed couples on Grand Designs, building a house out of recycled shipping containers that runs on garbage fumes, I very much doubt you're looking to live a life completely cut off from all forms of technology. You're not on the Interpol most wanted list (one hopes), so there's no reason to go completely off grid.

Instead, treat your digital detox as a set of lifestyle adjustments. Identify what habit would be the easiest to change and start from there. Notifications keeping you up at night? Turn off push. Going to dinner with friends? Try an hour or so on Airplane mode. Start with achievable minor changes before working your way up to the bigger gestures like deleting email accounts or locking yourself out of social media. Only you know yourself well enough to assess what you're capable of, so be sure to go with a plan that is well-paced and workable, rather than starting out by taking a pair of scissors to all of your cables.

② *Set a Timeframe*

A digital detox is not something that has some sort of indefinite timespan, starting from the moment you put your phone down and only ending on your deathbed. By its very definition, a detox is a 'process or period of time' – and not period like a lifetime or historical era.

Set a timeframe dependent on your objective – from having an unplugged weekend to cutting down social media use over a month. Whatever it is, go by the general rule that the longer the time, the less drastic the cut down. For example, two days without any social media use at all is realistic, but two months is bordering on impossible. For the latter period, you're likely to see more success with a detox plan that allows social media at the weekends, or predesignated internet browsing hours. Check out the different digital detox plans at the back of this book for timeframe-based ideas and suggestions.

③ *Make Clear Rules*

A digital detox is no time to be vague; if you want results, you have to be clear about what you can and cannot access. If you're not cutting things out entirely, stipulate what allowances you are permitting yourself: if you have to reply to emails, do so from 7 until 8. If you're still using Instagram, decide you can only scroll through your feed on your commute to work. Set your parameters. Not only will this keep you in check and on track, but having preset allowances will force you to be more productive and efficient, which in turn will help you develop healthier habits with technology.

④ *Be Prepared*

Behind every great effort is a mountain of preparation. You wouldn't start training for a marathon without running shoes and you wouldn't start a juice cleanse with a refrigerator completely devoid of juice. A digital detox is no different.

Each digital detox varies in its necessities but there will always be things to take care of before you begin (heads up: 99.9% of digital detoxes require an alarm clock, so you be sure to check that off of your list early). If you need to set an automatic response on your email, do it now. If you have a ton of emails to slog through for work, get them out of the way before you begin so you can start with a clearer headspace.

⑤ *Be Patient*

Think of a digital detox like a diet. No human on earth is immune to temptation, and whilst we may try our best to stave off the cravings, sometimes we can't help but give in and have a little cheat now and then. That's fine; just avoid the snowball effect. If you cave and check Facebook in the morning, don't write off the entire day. Don't let an error derail any of the progress you've been making.

One slip-up doesn't equate to total failure. Allow yourself to make mistakes and treat them as a learning experience. Work out what works best for you. Remember, you've grown up with technology at your fingertips; it's going to be difficult to readjust to a different routine day-to-day. Be patient with yourself and your progress throughout the process.

⑥ *Set Goals*

As aforementioned, a digital detox needs to have a clear end, and the path to the finish should be punctuated with objectives. Goals are an integral component of any digital detox; without them, you're essentially just testing your endurance, not making any real lifestyle changes or progress.

Ask yourself: what do you want to achieve from your detox? Maybe you want to have stronger boundaries between your workload and off-duty life. Perhaps you would like to be less dependent on your phone. Maybe you just want some more 'me time'. They're all valid desires and will dictate the shape your digital detox will take.

Having a target gives you a clear objective to work towards. It makes the whole process easier knowing it's to help realise something you want.

⑦ *State of Mind*

Like all things in life, your mindset has a huge effect on the outcome of any situation. A digital detox is no different. Think positive! Yes, detox means cutting things out, but don't try to life your life on a deficit, think of new (or even reintroduce some old) things to fill up the space in your new tech-lighter life.

As soon as you start thinking about it as some form of deprivation, the resentment will creep in and your likelihood to cave and given will increase tenfold. Just remember: replace, not remove.

(8) *Treat Yourself*

If you make it a day without looking at your phone, have a cupcake. Or an episode of Black Mirror. Or whatever floats your boat. Each to their own. Everything's more fun when treats are involved.

(9) *Be Productive*

When your fingers have become accustomed to drumming on a keyboard all day, you may find them drumming mindlessly on the table top as you find yourself with nothing to do now that your digital detox is in full swing.

If you're sitting on your sofa, blankly staring at a wall, of course you'll be more inclined to break and pick up your phone. Be productive with your time and keep yourself busy. Go outside. Meet friends. Read that book you've been meaning to pick up. Try... needlepoint? Remember: the devil makes work for idle hands (or thumbs).

▷ Baby Steps

• Starting Your Day Right

What's the first step of your morning routine? Do you hit the bathroom? Do you start considering what you're going to wear that day? Or do you pick up your phone, squint blearily into the inexplicably harsh brightness blaring into your feeble eyes and scroll through your notifications?

If your answer is the latter, your day begins the same as countless others across the world. A global study by Deloitte found that 61% of people check their phones within the first 5 minutes of waking up, 88% in the first 30 minutes, and 96% within the hour.[1] The 4% that resist checking their devices until after that 60-minute threshold? They rule over our world in an apex of efficiency and incomprehensible state of Zen.

Okay, not quite, but chances are they're having a more productive day than you are.

Mobile phones have replaced the newspaper in the ubiquitous morning catch up routine, but our devices provide way more information than the old paper and ink combo, and it's often extraneous and unnecessary for our brains to fumble around at first light. As useful as their (not always trusty, let's be honest) alarm functions are, our mornings would actually be much more productive without the help of any gadgets.

Your morning routine is key and putting your best foot forward really sets the tone for the rest of the day. You know what they say: begin as you mean to go on.

Take Control

If you look at your phone before you get out of bed, you – as dramatic as this sounds – are renouncing control of your mood. More often than not, your morning mindset frames the rest of your day, and checking your phone first thing means that mindset is created purely by reaction, not conscious decision.

Your mood is completely at the mercy of everything that happened when you were tucked up in your bed. Lucky you, if you are fortunate enough to wake up to a flood of likes and unexpected good news. But what if it's the opposite? It's difficult to have a good day when it began with news of governmental failure, or that your ex is in a new relationship.

You need to reclaim control of your day and make a conscious decision to start on a brighter note. Draw your curtains and look outside (apparently this is how people checked the weather before apps, I am told); even if it's only for a moment, it makes a much better first sight than the glare of a screen and a list of things you have missed.

When you wake up, try to engage in a simple activity that puts you in a good mood: whether it's listening to your favorite artist or an inspiring audiobook, or engaging in a little light yoga or meditation. Even just making the conscious effort to get up and make your bed. The key is to play an active role in your day's beginning, not a passive one.

Forwards, Not Backwards

When you start your morning routine by checking your notifications, you are bombarding your drowsy brain with a barrage of information before it has even fully woken up. Everything that you have missed whilst asleep – the good and the bad – must be acknowledged and processed; we are on the back foot before our eyes have even adjusted, already playing catch-up. In the words of Tristan Harris, Google's former Design Ethicist,

When we wake up in the morning and turn our phone over to see a list of notifications — it frames the experience of "waking up in the morning" around a menu of "all the things I've missed since yesterday."[2]

Looking through your notifications in the morning may seem harmless, but think about the measures we go to in order to avoid falling behind tasks or workflow during the day. By checking your phone first thing, you are unconsciously making the decision to start the day behind before it has even begun.

Your first thoughts should be forward-looking, not backwards. If you leave your phone untouched, think about how much time you'll have free.

Twenty to thirty minutes doesn't seem like much in the grander scheme of a day, but in a morning, it might as well be four hours. Use the time anywhere you need it (excluding bed, be strict) – a longer shower, actually sitting down to eat breakfast, or even taking a more scenic route to work.

The morning is the perfect time to be in tune with the moment, and the day ahead of you. Forget 5pm, the golden hour is between 7 and 8 am. This is prime time, when our brain is super receptive, which we never took advantage of before.

Making a to-do list for the day is a great practice to carry efficiency from the morning right throughout the day.

Tips for a Better Morning

Wake up to an alarm clock, or a radio alarm. If you can't get your hands on one and simply have to rely on a device to wake you up, try setting it up at the other side of the room from your bed. Getting up to turn it off will quash the urge to stay in bed and scroll through any notifications you missed while you were sleeping. You're also less likely to fall victim to the snooze/ten-more-minutes-timer trap; why have patchy batches of sleep and wake up groggy when you can kick off the day with a clear start?

Start small and work your way up: if you can't resist the lure of those pushy notifications, try no phone for 30 minutes, and then later 45 minutes, and then eventually an hour.

Develop new habits. If your hand automatically reaches for your phone, put something else in its place instead. Try a book on your bedside table to read a few pages before you get up, or maybe put your yoga mat closer your bed to prod you into doing some stretches.

• Ending Your Day Right

We all know about the importance of a good night's sleep. It's something that is preached to us from everywhere and everyone: parents, teachers, doctors, ourselves, in a soft whisper as we catch our reflection in the black screen between Netflix episodes with a tear of futile frustration rolling down our cheek.

And yet... one more episode couldn't hurt, right? One more Instagram check? And don't forget those WhatsApps and emails that should most definitely be replied to right now and not tomorrow morning. We're more likely to snuggle up to our screens than our teddy bears these days. Good night, sweet iPhone, sleep tight.

But the consequences of technology intruding our rest are not simply affecting our next-day productivity or giving us a cranky start. There are very serious health repercussions at risk when we start inviting our gadgets to bed with us.

"Checking your phone before you sleep is killing you!" I didn't mean to alarm you with this sudden extreme cry, but this is a real headline. A real, published headline. Yes, it's a destination we're all doomed for anyway, and there are lifestyle choices that are definitely going to get you there faster than some late-night Snapchat jaunts, but they certainly aren't helping matters.

Eyes Wide Open

Our eyes, again, are paying the price for our bad tech habits. The primary culprit? The bright blue light that smartphone and tablet screens emit, that is – as light tends to be – more pronounced in the dark, i.e. bed time. Close exposure to that light damages our retinas, which eventually leads to a gradual loss of centered vision.

On top of that, blue light has a huge effect on your hormonal production, too. In a natural setting, your body produces a hormone called melatonin, which essentially tells you that you're tired and it's time to call it a day. The blue light suppresses the production of melatonin, and essentially tells your brain to stay awake – that's why you toss and turn for about an hour after putting the screen away. Your brain is super wired and has been tricked into thinking it's the middle of the day; you've got a while before you manage to wind down again.

The Importance of Sleep

Disrupting your natural sleep cycle has some consequences heavier than dark circles beneath your eyes. Sleep maintains our physical and mental well-being. 7-8 hours are not recommended purely for us to feel well-rested, it's actually required for our brain to remain healthy.

We're preventing our bodies from cleaning house, essentially. When we rest, the supportive glial cells in our brains clean up toxins our neurons have emitted during the day. In turn, the chronic sleep disruptions caused by technology before bedtime can increase the risk for diseases like premature dementia and Alzheimer's.

Emotionally, disrupted sleep has been linked to depression; intellectually, it hinders focus and can exacerbate ADHD; and physically, it can result in increased blood pressure, a risk for diabetes and even hypertrophic remodeling. Of course, this is not an overnight issue. You're not going to spend all night on Facebook, sleep three hours as a result and wake up diseased. However, if this sleep-disruptive behavior goes on for years, then these health issues compound and become very real.

In short, improper rest affects us inside and out, and our infatuation with staring at a smartphone or tablet screen before bed is exacerbating a very serious problem. So put the gadget down: Twitter will still be there to read tomorrow morning.

Tips to End Your Day Right

Designate a window of time that ends at least one hour before you go to bed to take care of any emails or social media checks you need to make. Stick to your time frame; the sixty minutes of down time should be plenty of time for your mind to successfully unwind before you try to sleep.

Put your phone on Airplane mode before you go to sleep to avoid being awakened by any calls or notifications.

Keep your phone as physically far away from your bed as possible to eliminate the temptation of waking up and checking it during the night.

• A Digitally Minimalist Home

The home is becoming an increasingly digital space. Voice control is being incorporated into game consoles, refrigerators feature LED screens and the phrase 'autonomous robot vacuum cleaner' is an actual thing (hey, Roomba). In fact, with the dawn of smart devices like Amazon Alexa and Google Home being integrated into our home's technology, we are perhaps closer to requiring Isaac Asimov's Three Laws of Robotics for our household helpers than we may realise.

This has not been an overnight development, particularly not for millennials. We have grown up alongside the evolving digital home. With technology constantly within reach, we have never known a life without a screen in the living room, or a computer in the study.

We have not lived in a home like our grandparents did - a home without buttons and screens - and there is no reason for us to try to return to a state that we, ourselves, have never known. However, there are plenty of reasons for us to take a more minimalist approach and pare down some of the superfluous technology-use in an attempt to decelerate the breakneck speed with which we are hurtling towards I, Robot becoming a potential reality. Unplug and activate your digitally minimalist home.

The Bedroom

The bedroom is the first and most important place you should be aiming to 'cleanse', so to speak. Most of the technology we use in here is not necessary and can be easily replaced or removed for the space to more efficiently serve its purpose: rest. Sorting out this space can be a great first step in any digital detox.

And yet, removing devices from the bedroom is often met with the same pushback. One typical objection is how can you be expected to get up in the morning without your phone alarm? Well, back in the 19th century, a French inventor filed a patent on a mechanical alarm clock. If mankind managed to get themselves out of bed with one of those for two centuries before phone alarms became the norm, then you can too.

"But I need to watch TV or read my iPad or I can't fall asleep!" Yes, you can fall asleep without a screen's help; in fact, it's likely to be a much easier plight. If you need to unwind before you can doze off, an old-fashioned book is a better alternative and a much more sleep-conducive option.

A very easy, small step to take would be to designate your bed as a no-tech space. That means anywhere else in the room is A-OK, but there's strictly no screen allowed when you're tucked tight under your duvet. This should help stop you chronically lying to yourself when you say 'just one more episode' on Netflix, at least. Countless studies have shown that the artificial light exposure from screens makes it more difficult to fall asleep, so a device-less bed should facilitate a good night's rest.

The Living Room

Ah, the living room: the digital hub of the home. This is where it all began, with families gathered around, enraptured by the television's supreme rule. Dramatic, yes, but the dawn of the television really did kick off the domestic digital boom, and has long been the tent pole of the technological home. Other devices may have come and gone (goodbye, Betamax, we, uh, literally never knew ye), but the television has kept its place in the living room, with other, smaller devices huddling around it over time.

But there are plenty of other forms of entertainment besides the television. Instead of watching a TV show, sit back on the sofa and curl up with a good book. Maybe even dabble in something new; you'd be surprised at how fun an old-school game night can be with friends.

A good way to pare down on your devices in the living room is to operate under a one-screen-only policy. If you're watching TV, focus on that - do not have a laptop popped open or your phone nearby for idle scrolling. Likewise, if you're browsing the Internet on your computer, you do not need to have the television providing background noise. A single-screen rule is an easy and efficient way to minimise device usage.

The Kitchen

Okay, the approach to a digitally minimalist kitchen is by no means ripping microwaves out of the wall fittings or anything as drastic. No one is asking you to forgo the oven and crack out your firewood and matches. In fact, it has very little to do with your actual appliances and cooking practices, but rather your behavior in the space.

Try to start collecting cookbooks and recipes instead of trawling through the Internet to find something to make. It feels inexplicably more legitimate to pick up a book and follow a page as you prepare and cook ingredients, something that is somewhat lost in just glancing at and scrolling down a screen.

Additionally, if you eat in the kitchen, don't allow any phone use until the meal is over. That goes for you and your guests; keep your phone on a dock for ambient music if you must, but that's as much as that device should be allowed to contribute to your mealtime. If there's a TV in there, turn it off when you're eating and take the time to focus on your meal and reflect on your day, or make conversation, if there's company. Little changes like these will help make the kitchen less of a tech-heavy space.

The Bathroom

One would think that a room with that much water and condensation would naturally position itself as a firm no-go zone for digital devices, and yet here we are, in 2018, faced with some alarming statistics. In a study done by an online address-book site named Plaxo, more than 19% of phone owners have dropped their phone in the toilet.[1] 19%. Think of the five people you last spoke to – at least one of them has butterfingers'ed their phone into the porcelain abyss at one point.

If your phone manages to avoid the plunge, it has another delightful danger it must face: germs. And it doesn't matter how often you spray that Dettol, bathroom surfaces are teeming with bacteria by default - and that's not even considering the horrors that await you in public restrooms. There are so many chances of contaminating your device, does it not kind of null the whole washing your hands thing if you're then picking up a filthy phone and pressing it against the side of your face later?

So why, according to Verizon, are 90% people bringing their phones into the bathroom?[2] People have claimed they're avoiding boredom, others that they don't want to miss any important messages whilst they're... otherwise occupied. I mean, there's multi-tasking, and then there's... well, texting from the toilet. Don't be that person.

If it's not already, declare your bathroom the one non-negotiable gadget free zone in your entire home. Your phone is still going to be there when you're done. There is nothing in this world that can't wait the two or three minutes you need in there. Nothing.

• Technology and Relationships

Technology is an essential part of how we perceive relationship maintenance in today's modern world. It allows us to keep in touch with new, unprecedented ways that are constantly evolving. First, the phone call. Now, video call. What will it be in the future? The sky is truly the limit.

Digital devices are consistently reducing the effort that relationships once required. Letters do not need to be scratched upon parchment by an ink-dipped quill and sealed with wax by candle-light. Okay, that may have been a good few hundred years back of a comparison, but think how far technology has allowed us to come with communication convenience. We can email a coworker an update, Skype a parent from the other side of the world, send a quick photo to a loved one or tag a friend in a meme without any comment at all. All these methods of communication contribute to our countless relationships and would be impossible without our various gadgets. We are continuously connected with every single person we have ever met – and even people we haven't – and have the ability to strike up a conversation with any of them at any moment, all at our fingertips.

But we wield a double-edged sword, and it cuts both ways. Whilst technology facilitates relationships in overcoming the obstacle of distance, you may be less aware of how it is inadvertently disrupting our relationships closer to home.

Virtual vs. Reality

The relationship between technology and relationships is almost as difficult to wrap your head around as this very sentence. It gives with one hand and takes away with the other, and when it takes away, it does so with all the stealth and silence of a well-seasoned hitman. We seem to be completely oblivious to the detriments of turning to tech during real-time interactions. Whether it's a friend, a family member, or a loved one, can we ever truly focus on each other when digital devices are to hand? We compulsively check our screens mid-conversation and think nothing of it; no objection, no apology, and often not even an acknowledgment.

'So what?' You may be saying, thinking of one relationship in particular. 'Yeah, we check our phones when we're together, but we're totally comfortable with that.' Yes, you may both be okay with that dynamic – it is, after all, never really all that frowned upon; in fact, it's often heralded as 'goals' to hit that level of comfort – but you may also be unaware of the negative effects that digital dependency has on our behavior within relationships:

- We prioritize online conversations and networks over real ones.

- Our focus has switched from sharing the experience with those around you to sharing the perfect capture with those online.

- We are not present or truly in the moment together.

Mobile phones provide us with unlimited access to a wider virtual social network than our physical reality. It is difficult to resist the lure of a push notification and more often than not, in the presence of others, we do not even make an attempt to do so. We have become conditioned to consistently engage with our wider-networked relationships to the detriment of interactions occurring in real time.

'Are You Done?': Something to Think About

Imagine that every conversation you have on your phone is with a person physically next to you. If you're having a real face-to-face interaction with someone, would you be okay interrupting that conversation to physically turn away and talk to someone else? Would you be okay if someone did that to you mid-sentence? What if every interruption was prefaced (and thus highlighted) with "are you finished?" or "oh, hold on, one second..."? You'd be quicker to call that behavior rude, but is answering and sustaining other conversations on our phones whilst with others all that different? We regularly engage in this behavior, but it's somehow accepted because there is no one else physically present, and the interruptions are not verbally acknowledged.

Being so connected online is distracting us from connecting with each other. A study found that mobile phones – whether they're being used or even just visibly present – prevent the development of closeness and trust between individuals.[1] The mere presence of a mobile phone means that any moment between you and another person can be interrupted at any point by, essentially, anyone else on the planet. Our dependence on digital devices is both hindering the development of new relationships and debilitating our current ones.

Signs Your Relationship Needs a Digital Detox

- Long periods of time are spent on separate gadgets and not talking, either typing away on laptops or scrolling through newsfeeds. It's an amicable silence, but a silence nonetheless.

- You've noticed that conversations – or even sentences – have been interrupted by you or someone else checking a phone.

- When you go for a meal or a coffee, you sit down and put your phone on the table before you even look at the menu or start

- talking to each other.

- You know what they've been up to thanks to their social media feeds as opposed to actually hearing it from them directly.

- You've wondered who they're talking to (not in an 'I'm-about-to-hire-a-PI' suspicious way but just out of curiosity) or what they're so busy looking at or typing, and been aware of waiting for them to finish for you to continue.

Two's Company

A digital detox may be a good idea to disconnect from the online social sphere and reconnect with someone. Whether you have identified the problematic symptoms in yourself or in both of you, why not consider trying one out together? It wouldn't hurt to add a little accountability to your task. A digital detox does not need to be a solo venture. In fact, it may be a lot of easier to tackle with a partner or two by your side.

You can even make a game out of it. Go out for dinner and put your phones in a pile (face-down, obviously) on the table. Whoever checks their phone throughout the duration of the night has to pick up the check. If you want to keep the game-aspect up even when you're not together, certain apps can make a detox a fun challenge. Download ShutApp with a friend (or a group) and designate times that you agree to not use your phone. As soon as someone caves and picks their phone up, everyone will be alerted. Choose fun prizes or forfeits to keep things interesting.

With a digital detox buddy, you can navigate the tech-free waters with the support of someone else by your side. When things get hard, turn to them: make a pact to write each other letters instead of constantly texting, ask them about their day instead of scrolling through a newsfeed, or if you feel your fingers itching for the feel of a keyboard beneath them, see if they want to go for a walk or visit a museum. There's a plentitude of fun, non-tech-orientated activities to do on a digital detox, and they can only be more enjoyable with some pleasant company. This is a chance for you to make new discoveries with someone special and leave the devices at home. Just you, them and some dedicated time.

• Apps to Cop and Drop

I know, I know – downloading technology to facilitate a technology detox, how ironic. It may seem counter-productive but at the end of the day, these apps can help you become less dependent on your digital devices in a way that a pen, paper and a prayer simply can't.

COP Moment | Platform: iOS

Why it's a keeper:

Moment is the very first app you should be getting your hands on before you start any form of digital detox. The app helps you track your mobile phone usage by not only telling you how many times you've picked up your phone, but also how long you've spent on it.

It even gets into the nitty-gritty and tells you how long on each individual app. Sure, it's not always easy to see you've spent a collective 50 minutes of screen time swiping on Tinder, but sometimes that's the harsh truth you need to face to spur some change.

OFFTIME | Platform: Android

Why it's a keeper:

OFFTIME is similar to Moment in that you can track your device usage and habits, but you can also set periods of time to block calls, texts and notifications from everyone that's not on your approved list (which means you don't need to worry about missing any important calls).

UNROLL.ME | Platform: iOS / Android / Online

Why it's a keeper:

Clearing out your mailbox so you're only receiving top priority messages is a must for any successful detox. Unroll.me accesses your email inbox and collates all of your email subscriptions into a single list; you can see all of them at once and unsubscribe from any with a simple click.

ANTI-SOCIAL | Platform: Desktop

Why it's a keeper:

Anti-social is simple in its premise and use: just plug in the URLs you want to block yourself from and how long you'd like the plugin to keep them off limits. There's no takebacks, so be sure you're ready when you hit 'OK'.

SHUTAPP – DIGITAL DETOX | Platform: iOS

Why it's a keeper:

ShutApp just adds a little fun challenge to digital detoxing. Download it with a friend and set a time that you both don't want to use your phone. You'll be notified if your friend caves and picks up, and vice versa.

Drop

When it comes to culling, it doesn't help to think of specific apps so much as it does to think of *types* of apps. It's time to say goodbye to any app that falls into the following categories.

Distractors

Game apps like puzzles and free-runners exist purely to get you on your phone and keep you on your phone. They're built to distract you with mindless tapping as you wait in the queue for your venti at Starbucks. Cut.

Dating Apps

I know it's a wild notion to make such a suggestion, but why not try meeting someone… in person? Give the old-fashioned way a try.

Flexing Social Media

Okay, not all social media needs to be culled; some platforms have become integral for business, or even just for keeping in touch with relatives. Any social media sites that exist purely to flex have got to go. No one needs to see your new trainers on a 5 second loop. No one needs to see your dinner under a Valencia filter. Snapchat, Twitter, musical.ly, goodbye.

Out of Office

Any app that ties you to the office when you're not sitting at your desk needs to be deleted, or at least be put on cool down. If it's too much to get rid of completely, put a timer boundary on it, set an automatic out of office reply or at least turn off the notifications.

Delivery Apps

Even picking up the phone and calling is preferable; it's still a tech-enabled process, but at least you're interacting with another human being.

Shopping Apps

99% of the time, a shopping app's utility can easily be supplanted by you just going to a physical store and shopping in person. If it's a purely online retailer, then stick to visiting the website via your computer to cut down on your usage.

HOW TO
SURVIVE

▷ **The Mindset**

With all lifestyle changes, your mental approach is key to your success or failure. For a digital detox, you are inevitably headed for defeat if you allow a vacuum to exist where technology once occupied your life. It will take on a form similar to a black hole, slowly drawing in and destroying its surroundings on its unstoppable path of carnage.

A digital detox is the same as any other attempt to purge toxicity. When we remove anything from our lives - be it a bad habit (like smoking), a food group (goodbye, carbs), or even a person (like You Know Who) - we do not just create a void in the space it once filled. We are more likely to succeed in any endeavor by replacing the negative with something positive. We use electronic cigarettes, we eat zucchini pasta (okay, it'll never be the same, but it serves the point I'm making) and we refocus on healthy relationships or try to meet someone new. A digital detox should be no different. Keep your hands busy, keep your brain stimulated.

Don't remove - replace.

When you approach a digital detox from a place of replacement instead of removal, it becomes a much easier path to walk. There are two main senses of 'replacement' that will serve you well: the macro and the micro.

On a macro level, a detox should replace the digital clutter and jumble in your life with the ability to renew, reconnect and recalibrate. A digital detox is not really about checking your email less, or being less attached to your phone. Those are just symptoms of success. The real goal is to retool your mindset to engineer a new, more efficient approach to your decision-making and thus, your lifestyle. You are replacing waste with productivity.

On a micro level, you should be thinking about replacing your bad tech habits with healthier, more productive alternatives. You would be surprised at how much of a time-suck mindless technology use builds up to be: Facebook check ups, Instagram posts, Wikipedia deep dives, they all really add up. With these gone and more time on your hands, you should be thinking of new practices to pick up in their absence.

The key to achieving any enduring, effective behavioral change is to frame it positively. As soon as you get away from thinking about losing things - missing out, putting down, any form of removal - and start thinking about what you stand to gain, your digital detox will not only be that much easier to get through, but that much more rewarding when you complete it.

The Power of Positivity

It sounds trite but you shouldn't underestimate the power that positive thinking has on something like a digital detox. A mind full of positive thoughts is empowering, and ultimately your best support through a process like this.

If you slip up, do not berate yourself. Negative thoughts can quickly pile up and spiral into an energy-wasting snowball that can derail your efforts. One mistake is not total failure. Think positively: now you have identified a weakness that you can work harder to address, fix and move on from.

Take any obstacle you face on this tech-lite escapade as an opportunity to learn more about yourself. Make the best of things; stay positive.

▷ Beating Procrastination and Being Productive

Allow me to show my age for a moment. When I was younger, I would watch The Amanda Show most days after school. One of the sketches featured a character called the Procrastinator, with the catchphrase: "I'll get to it… eventually!" The Procrastinator was a superhero in a (questionably) skin-coloured bodysuit that would delay saving the fire department from a fire (top quality comedy, I'm sure you can tell) to listen to a new CD or finish a bologna sandwich. The amusement lay in the - wildly exaggerated - premise that someone could put off something so urgent for something so menial. Triviality trumping urgency was presented as a form of absurdist comedy. Ha ha ha, you were supposed to say, this is funny because her priorities are very skewed. This would never happen in real life.

And yet today, I found myself in the middle of a project on deadline day, watching a video of a girl in weird sunglasses making a tribute to the Goosebumps theme song (a true classic if you haven't seen it, by the by).

Technology: it gives and it takes. Whilst it is designed to enhance our lives with convenience, some is undeniably designed to encourage our minds to wander. Technology can induce a somewhat unconscious state of engagement that we are often only aware of slipping into a good ten or fifteen minutes in, if at all.

With so many digital distractions available at our finger tips, the Procrastinator's catchphrase rings true with us all: we'll get to it… eventually.

Goodbye, Attention Span

A plethora of digitally driven stimulation bombards us from all directions; we have never been more distracted as we are in today's digital age. It is becoming harder and harder for our minds to focus on a singular task from inception to completion.

With a world of options at our fingertips, our cognitive control is wearing thin. Microsoft released a study that linked our increasingly tech-heavy lifestyle to our deteriorating attention spans, which now sits at around eight seconds on average - shorter than that of a goldfish.[1] Next time someone tells you that you have the attention span of a goldfish, they're unknowingly inferring your attention span is one second longer than the average human's. You better take that compliment and run with it.

This is not an issue we are oblivious to; we know all too well that technology distracts us from tasks at hand. We've all been there: a quick check to identify that actress whose face you recognize from somewhere somehow ends up forty minutes later looking at a list of animals with fraudulent diplomas on Wikipedia. But this doesn't happen because you're weak minded or a slave to curiosity; former Google designer and ethicist Tristan Harris writes in great detail about how technology is literally designed to hijack our minds and psychological vulnerabilities. We are all too aware that we are designing technology in a borderline predatory sense, and yet all too often finding ourselves falling prey.

And then we have the distractions we are oblivious to. Think about what you're really picking up with your digital device: email, texting, phone calls, and not to mention the countless iterations of social networking sites and apps. We are constantly multi-tasking without ever really being aware of it, dealing with an inundation of tasks that are impossible to complete sequentially, or even definitively. Technology makes it very easy for us to shift from task to task without having to ever really finish anything.

How to Boost Your Productivity

So how can we reclaim control and boost our productivity in a world of technological temptation? We will always be prone to lapses in focus, but there are small behavioral changes you can make to lessen your exposure to digital distractions and help keep yourself on track.

Enable a little bit of Parental Control on yourself. If you have something to do, block access to sites that you know will do their best to lure you out of focus mode. You can also find similar services to block apps on your phone.

Try to focus on singular tasks instead of mutli-tasking. Think of an 'open' and a 'close', and do not allow yourself to move on until you can 'close' a task.

Stop opening fifty tabs on your computer. Take the information you need and copy it into a file to refer to later if need be, but don't just leave them open and piling up. Only keep windows open that are relevant to the task at hand and you'll be less likely to find yourself dipping in and out.

Be strategic. If you have a larger task ahead, schedule out your time to avoid wandering off task. Be sure to factor breaks into your schedule too, to allow your brain time to rest, but within a set time limit to prevent procrastinating.

Find an accountability buddy. Tell them what your progress goals are for a certain task and keep them up to date - you'll be less likely to find yourself on that girl you hated in high school's Facebook if you have to explain to someone else where you were spending all that time you wasted.

▷ Staying Social Without Social Media

If a tree falls in a forest and no one is around to hear it, does it make a sound?

If the perfect chia breakfast bowl was set upon a marble tabletop without a photograph, did you even eat it? I get it, growing up as a millennial, social media plays a hugely important role in our lives. Our daily routines are perforated with its different forms; Tweeting out a thought to the masses, liking someone's post as a sign of acknowledgment, or selecting the right the filter to present a carefully prepared snapshot of our day.

Our biggest fear of disconnecting from social media is ultimately disconnecting from our relationships within its network. There's no shame in it, because it's ultimately the most human of fears - the fear of being forgotten. But embarking on a digital detox and taking a break from social media should not have to mean taking a break from being social.

The Fear of Missing Out

Anxiety that an exciting or interesting event may currently be happening elsewhere, often aroused by posts seen on social media. (OED)

The fear of missing out (more snappily abbreviated to FOMO) on some sort of rewarding experience or similar is not a new social anxiety, but it is certainly one that is aggressively aggravated by the pervasiveness of social media today. Our constant need to stay connected to social networks is a symptom of FOMO, as is our desire to keep everyone updated - via text or images - with our lives.

For a lot of people, a digital detox is often associated with isolation, but that does not have to be the case. You are not locking yourself in a room with nothing but a book, a candle and your own company. A digital detox does not need to interfere with your day-to-day life. What is it exactly that you fear missing out on? All of those Tweets, all of those photos, all of your devices; they're still going to be there when you're allowed to pick them up again. They are not transient forms of content; the Internet is forever (as you have been warned, several times I'm sure). Social media should not be your sole form of social interaction. Relationships do not need to be – and certainly shouldn't be - put on ice because of a digital detox.

Disconnect, Reconnect

Taking a step back from social media during a digital detox will make the quality (or lack thereof) of the connections you have in your life very clear. Sometimes it is difficult to assess our relationships when all it takes to engage is a double tap, but the truly valuable relationships we have should be able to exist - no, not simply exist, they should be able to flourish in the absence of social media. If you lose touch with a person because you have disappeared from their newsfeed, it is perhaps not a connection worth your effort to foster.

True connections can only be enriched without the crutch of social media. A digital detox is actually a really great way to get the most out of being social, allowing you to engage without the worry of digital distractions. You can truly interact with someone, and be present in the moments that you are creating together. You'll be surprised how little you're actually missing out on without your phone in your hand.

The Smaller Picture

Even though you have disconnected from social media, there are still ways to connect with those around you. You can still share without a designated button to click. When you post on social media, you are 'talking at', putting something out there to everyone and seeing who'll bite. We need to 'talk to', communicating with a specific person and refocusing on engagement and interaction.

If you find an interesting quote or a news article is riling you up, instead of retweeting or reposting, send it to someone whose opinion you'd like to hear. An interesting discussion (or vent) is infinitely more rewarding than a few likes of agreement.

Instead of blasting out a photo of your aesthetically pleasing lunch to the masses, send it to a foodie friend, or someone you'd want to revisit the restaurant with.

If you're feeling like tweeting out Drake lyrics at 2am because you're having 'a moment' (hey, we've all been there), think about reaching out to someone and talking about how you feel as opposed to making a passive aggressive jab via Canada's greatest wordsmith.

Staying social without social media is a perfectly achievable task, and is ultimately more rewarding without the crutch that social networking sites provide us with. Without social media, we can focus on the quality of our relationships and communication. If you truly are afraid of missing out on something without social media, chances are it isn't worth your worry; less is more, after all.

HOW TO
THRIVE

▷ Taking the Lead

Technology has been so ubiquitous in our society that it has created two very distinct identities: our real life and our digital presence. At the start, our real life was very much the dominant entity, but as social media evolved, the scale tipped. Our digital presence has become integrated with our real life, in an almost omniscient sense. It has changed how we go about our day and how we view the present. With constant social media updates in the form of photos, stories, and Tweets, we have made an inadvertent shift from participants to storytellers and observers.

Without realizing, we have ultimately become the narrator of our own lives instead of the main character. Our focus is not on experiencing the moment but rather relating it to others via some form of digital media. We would rather filter, edit and present a moment as opposed to being in it, and digital devices are the tools we use to do so. They have become our pen and paper; integral in shaping the narrative we are so intent on controlling.

Technology may have created this shift, but we have all the power of reclaiming the lead role in our lives. We do not have to be crafters if we readjust our focus to the present moment, and not the digital network surrounding us.

We need to prioritize real life, which sounds obvious, but is something we unconsciously neglect to do. I admit: I am guilty of looking out aesthetically pleasing cafés and inviting a friend with the sole premise of taking photos for our Instagram feeds. We're both aware of the intent behind the outing - which, perhaps, is even worse - and perfectly okay with it. Within moments of arriving, shots are set up, 'candid' poses are hit and we're snapping away.

Of the countless photos, maybe one or two make the cut to filtering stage - another long and arduous process. Looking back at my Instagram profile now, I can recall setting up the picture and the angles we were trying to hit, but I don't really remember what my friend and I spoke about that day, or how the red velvet cake tasted.

I know I am by no means the only person guilty of this behavior, but confronting its existence when writing this has been somewhat wince inducing. What an incredibly unhealthy approach to social interaction, in which we are making real life a mere vehicle to our digital identities. We need to tip the balance so that social media is an afterthought, not a cause. Moments should be organic, not engineered. We shouldn't be creating real-life experiences to enhance our social media presence; if we embrace life and take the lead, then those moments should happen on their own.

▷ The Importance of Doing Nothing

'Idle brains are the devil's workhouses.' [1] - T. Fuller, 1732

This proverb has been through countless iterations and adjustments throughout history but its core sentiment has endured. Yes, we may have graduated from the idea of 'sin' being the condemnable result of inactivity but the gist is the same: an idle mind is a wasted mind, and an undesirable state of mind to be in.

However, over time, the notion has developed that a single task is not suffice to occupy the mind. Multi-tasking has become such an intrinsic part of our day-to-day routines that you would be hard pushed to think of one activity to which we wholly devote ourselves, and whilst this is by no means a modern problem, the prevalence of technology has undoubtedly exacerbated it. In fact, technology has unconsciously allowed our multi-tasking mindset to infiltrate even our moments of relaxation: we sit in front of the television, browsing through ASOS on our laptops or mindlessly scrolling through our Instagram feeds. A trip to the museum becomes a double act of enjoying the experience and finding the perfect frame and filter to capture it in. An open tab has at least three more behind it, waiting to be switched to at any moment. Think for a moment: when was the last time you sat down to watch a movie, or a program, without your phone beside you?

With multi-tasking as our default approach, we have neglected the wonders of inactivity. Yes, we regularly champion the importance of sleep (even if we don't always take heed) and think little of booking week-long vacations to recharge after a hard few months, but the most important breaks – yet the hardest to make time for – are smaller, regular breaks throughout the day; spaces of mental freedom that come from talking a walk, meditating, or drinking a latte in a café.

We have been conditioned to believe that breaks are for the weak or for the lazy, with little room for variation, but these small moments of downtime are essential. Studies have shown that in order for us to operate optimally, we should be taking breaks every 90-minutes of uninterrupted focus and work.[2] These smaller breaks are already scarce in today's culture, but they are also now technologically layered moments that seem to have at least one screen present at all times.

But not doing anything has become such a taboo that the idea of allowing time for, well, nothing, is something that doesn't even occur to us anymore. Doing nothing is seen as irresponsible - hence the prevalence of to-do lists - and a waste of 'valuable' time. But doing nothing is just as, if not more so, 'valuable' as working to achieve your goals. They go hand-in-hand, and ultimately, it is all the more difficult to achieve the latter without the former.

Embracing Nothing

'Learning without reflection is a waste, reflection without learning is dangerous.' [3] - Confucius

In our hyper-networked world, introspection and reflection are becoming lost practices because we are not allowing any time for them. Doing nothing is an invaluable opportunity for the brain to work unconsciously. It is a time for reflection in all of its possible forms. Allow your mind to wander over something you read or learnt, an interaction you had or a goal you wish to achieve. Let your mind process the thoughts it has without setting up other points of distraction. In Psychology Today, Ray William writes that:

Resting state neural networks help us process our experiences, consolidate memories, reinforce learning, regulate our attention and emotions, and keep us productive and effective in our work and judgments.[4]

True reflection and analysis can only be done without the multiple streams of data - conversations, sights, sounds - that it must focus on during our daily routines.

At the moment, our designated mental downtime is often only sleep, and even that is a process that gets habitually whittled down to compensate for more work. When we sleep, our brain is perhaps at its most active, but not in the same sense that it is during the day. Without actively focusing or engaging with the external world, the brain processes freely, unoccupied. Our wildest dreams are formed. Memories are revisited. Data is fortified. We awaken with consolidated information and subconsciously formulated thoughts and ideas. Sir Paul McCartney said that *Yesterday* came to him in a dream: *'I woke up with a lovely tune in my head. I thought, 'That's great, I wonder what that is?'*[5]

Imagine, then, what the brain could achieve if we allowed it more time to process subconsciously? Why must we limit this thought process to our dwindling sleep time? Making a point to set aside time for your brain to relax during the day allows our attention to turn inwards. For creatives, this is when the best ideas are formulated.

There's a reason why some of our most celebrated creative minds - from Beethoven to Steve Jobs - took daily walks to allow ideas to germinate. Your walk may not result in a world-class symphony or a global technology giant, but who know what ideas or revelations you may stumble across when you allow your mind to clear?

Even in writing this, the time I took to sit back and literally stare aimlessly out of the window proved just as integral to this chapter's fruition as the time I spent reading and researching. Embracing bouts of nothingness allows reflection, analysis and new focus.

• The Importance of Doing Nothing

Meditation is not rocket science, and whilst it may be an intimidating practice to approach, it is actually surprisingly simple; the key is to start small and build up. All you require is five minutes, just five, in which you can tune out.

Meditation doesn't require a yoga mat, an anatomically concerning pose or the soft sound of trickling water and panpipes. All you need to do is to stop whatever you're doing and breathe. Focus on the flow of your breath – in and out – and nothing else. When a thought slips into your mind, acknowledge it and pass it over. The more you practice, the easier emptying your mind becomes and the longer you can go without becoming distracted.

If meditation is too much of an ask, just take a step back. Put your phone down. Look away from your computer screen. Sit back in your chair. Go for a walk. Look out the window. Mental downtime is invaluable, regardless of its form.

Those who require it the most will find it the most difficult to fit in, so prioritize it: use alarms, set reminders, don't let yourself get snowballed with work and force yourself to stop for even just a moment. Let your mind wander. Dare to daydream.

▷ Reintegrating Technology

Okay, so perhaps you have come this far, identified some behaviors in yourself that you want to change and have embarked on a digital detox. You've made some big steps in cutting down your technology use, but detox plans are to be executed over an isolated period of time, not adopted for life. The detox period is over; what now? What is life post-digital detox?

The fact of the matter is that technology is not going anywhere. We cannot - and do not want to, quite frankly - revert back to life pre-technology, and we're more likely to die out before it does (and if you've ever seen any sci-fi movie set in a dystopian future, an inoffensively handsome, brunette teen will be humankind's only hope). If we want to be an active member of society in the 21st century, living completely free of technology is not an option.

But we do not need to take such a black or white, 0 or 100 approach when it comes to using technology. There is a healthy way to combine our real lives and our digital ones. It's all about striking that balance.

Mindfulness

A mental state achieved by focusing one's awareness on the present moment, while calmly acknowledging and accepting one's feelings, thoughts, and bodily sensations. (OED)

Practicing mindfulness may sound like an intimidating, somewhat abstract task, but in truth, it's just trying to be conscious and aware, i.e. exercising a little bit of focus. In fact, this is our natural state; it's just that now we live in a time with an unprecedented amount of technology-driven distractions. As technology evolves, we become more and more overwhelmed with stimulations. But technology is never going to stop evolving. We have to be the ones to take conscious action to reclaim our focus, and all it requires is a simple step back.

One pause, one thought, just one moment of clear consciousness: that makes all the difference. It's so easy to fall into a mindless state with our devices, but if we stay focused, we can continue to use them healthily. 'But how?' I know, it does sound very new-age and abstract, but it's not about actually telling yourself to focus so much as it's teaching yourself to do so through little behavioral changes. 'Like what?'

One easy practice would be to turn off auto-correct. Okay - bear with me, I know that's a controversial shout to make, but think about it for a moment: how much do you rely on your device editing your communication? Do you even really think about what you're writing anymore, knowing your phone can just clean it up, often haphazardly with some wild leaps in interpretation? Is it really such a big ask to turn it off and actually think about what we want to say to communicate?

And we don't need to banish our phones to our pockets any time we're out and about either. Yes, take a photo of a moment you wish to capture and share, but mindful technology use means saving the filter, the edit, the caption and the upload for later so you can continue enjoying the moment while you're in it. Embrace the #latergram, don't interrupt the present.

Out With the Old, In With the New

1. So the key to mindful technology use is to let go of your old, forgiving tech habits and developing some new ones that passively encourage focus. You know yourself better than anyone, so your own assessment of your behavior is key to identifying what needs to change and how, but here are five general, easy, healthier tech habits to consider picking up post-digital detox.

2. Let it Ring. If you're out with a friend or in any social situation, let your phone ring out if a call comes in. For allowances, make a mental list of three people that are must pick-ups. If it's anyone other than those select three? That's what voicemail's for, amigo.

3. Out of Office. Sometimes your job demands that ignoring your email in the evenings or at the weekend is impossible, but there's still a way to stay connected professionally without letting business intrude your personal life. Designate a window of time (no more than an hour) for evenings and weekends that you're allowed to deal with work emails, but outside of those windows, try to keep business correspondence during office hours.

4. Push Back. Social media is often the biggest culprit of distracting us, so an easy step you should be taking is to disable push notifications so you're only checking your feeds when you want to, not because you're being prompted. On top of that, keep your friends list culled down so when you do log in, you're only seeing things you have consciously decided to be important and relevant.

5. Check Yourself Before You Wreck Yourself. Be conscious of

how you're using your computer during your free time. At the end of the week, have a peek at your Internet history. Confronting, I know, but you can see where you're spending most of your time. Hindsight is 20/20. Ask yourself whether the time spent on recurring sites has been productive, and try to cut down on those that don't make the cut.

6. Work With the Enemy. Technology can actually support your new tech-lite habits, too. Check out the 'Apps to Cop and Drop' section of this book to find apps like Moment that can help you monitor and assess your device usage.

DIGITAL DETOX PLANS TO TRY

There is no one-size-fits-all digital detox; a successful digital detox is all about the individual, so don't be afraid to take a plan and shake some things up to find out what works best for you. Our plans in this chapter are great starting points to discovering your optimum tech-free life.

▷ One Weekend

A tech-free weekend is a totally feasible endeavor that doesn't ask for any huge lifestyle shifts right off the bat, or require a whole lot of preparation. That's why it's the perfect way to dip your toe and test out the digital detox waters. It's also an easy litmus test to judge your next step: if the weekend went without a hitch and wasn't too much of a hassle, why not try stepping it up to a week? If it was a difficult two days, maybe go back and amend your plan and give your edited weekend plan a spin with some more allowances now that you know what worked and what didn't.

48 hours: one small step for man, one giant leap for a pending stress-free, analog lifestyle.

Goal:

Unplug. Relax. Reset. Two days isn't too long, so you can really take quite a large step back from technology over a weekend. Focus on yourself and indulge, whilst setting the tone for the upcoming week.

Prep:

Tech-less weekends are generally non-invasive and require little prep, but it's always a good idea to let people know in advance that you're going device free if you're worried about missing important messages or inadvertently blanking a friend. If you've made already plans, be sure to tell whoever you're meeting that you'll be doing a detox and it'd be best to reach you via phone call if there are any changes in your plans.

It won't help to go in blind, so take allocate some time on Friday evening to reply to work emails or do some last-minute prep for the weekend ahead, like printing off recipes or researching afternoon activities.

If you're relying on your phone's alarm to wake you up tomorrow, set it up at the other side of your room, or as far from your bed as possible. Before you go to sleep, be sure to put it on Airplane Mode (or disable all of your push notifications, if you still want to receive phone calls) so you won't fall into the notifications trap when you turn off your alarm in the morning.

The Plan

Saturday Morning:

Start your morning off with some stretches, be it yoga, Pilates, or even just a little attempt at touching your toes. Stretching for 10-15 minutes in the morning is a great way to warm up your body for the day, but since you have way more free time on a Saturday morning than a busy weekday, really take the time to indulge in a good stretch; heading out for an early yoga or Pilates class is a great way to kick off the weekend.

Saturday Afternoon:

Keeping yourself busy is key for day one, and there are a simple five words you must abide by to succeed: get out of the house.

Instead of browsing online for a new jacket, why not go window-shopping? The whole process of shopping has changed so much now that almost every retailer has its own individual app but there's still nothing quite like the traditional shopping experience.

You might have forgotten what it's like to be able to try before you buy without having to fill out a returns slip, look out the box tape and organize a courier to come pick up your unwanted package.

Shopping's not everyone's idea of a fun few hours, but there's a plentitude of other activities to keep you busy. Go to a museum. Visit a bookstore. Head to the great outdoors and try a hike or a bike ride. The possibilities are endless; choose an activity you can throw yourself into without wondering what meals your friends are taking artful shots of.

Saturday Evening:

Instead of reaching for your food delivery app, why not try cooking something at home? If you're short for inspiration, avoid hitting up Pinterest and take a stroll down to your supermarket, or try inviting a friend over to make something together. If neither of you are particularly culinary-inclined, then head out to a restaurant with a little spontaneity; who cares if you can't check the Yelp reviews beforehand? Head somewhere that's caught your eye or you've always wanted to try.

Sunday Morning:

Sunday mornings are always the easiest part of any weekend detox because you've proved you can beat the first-day jitters. Now we're in cruise control. Allow yourself a lie-in, have breakfast in bed, read a magazine and just chill out.

Sunday Afternoon:

Now's the time to do something you've been putting off for a while. This will keep your mind focused on a task and off any missed notifications. It can be anything from clearing out your wardrobe, giving your home a good clean or even finally painting that accent wall. Getting something done will put a real productive spin on your weekend.

Sunday Evening:

Wind down with a glass of wine and indulge in some 'me' time. Grab the book you've always meant to start, or pick up a pen to jot down some ideas. It's also a good idea to take this time to soft-plan your upcoming week.

You don't need to be scheduling out all of your appointments with iCal style precision but think more along the lines of overarching aims or you want to achieve during the week.

It can even be something as trivial as what outfits you're going to wear or what you're going to cook for dinner. Getting into the habit of putting time aside to plan in advance is a nice way to end the weekend and set yourself up for a stress-free week.

Post-Plan Analysis

What to do if it worked out:

If this is your first digital detox, then congratulations are in order, first and foremost. Any lifestyle change is difficult to implement, and you've made a great first step in doing so. Now looking forward: this plan isn't supposed to be an every weekend, 5:2 kind of set up, but rather something you can turn to anytime you feel like you'd benefit from a good unplug. If you want to push things a little further, consider a seven-day digital detox, which is a more gradual, but longer, process.

What to do if it didn't work out:

Do not despair; you've got to walk before you can run. Try out these adjustments and give the weekend plan another go:

- Schedule an hour to flip open your laptop or use your phone. Where the hour falls is entirely up to you; pick whenever you felt the most prone to breaking. Whatever time you choose, be strict with yourself and stick to the hour you've allocated.

- Missing out on capturing memories or beautiful shots with your camera? If you can't invest in a camera, keep your phone on Airplane mode but take it with you so you can still snap away.

- Ask a friend to hang out with you over the weekend and try it together. Everything's easier with a helping hand.

▷ One Week

So you've graduated from the weekend program and are ready to push things a little further; welcome to the slightly-bigger-leagues of the seven day digital detox.

Goal:

Going off-grid for a weekend is a realistic ask, but attempting that for seven days would be a mean feat for even the most determined. Cold turkey is not the game to play here; approach a seven-day digital detox with particular focus on the linguistic definition of 'detox', a process in which you gradually rid yourself of (technological) toxicity.

Prep:

Since this is more of a gradual process, you won't require as much prep as the weekend plan as most of the changes will be made during the week itself. The only recommendation would be since this is a longer commitment than two days, try to purchase an alarm clock or radio alarm to wake you up. These relics haven't quite reached the museum yet, so maybe order one online before you're ready to start.

The Plan

Day 1: <u>Analog AM</u>

Start your week off with a tech-free morning that caps when you hit the office. This is primarily targeted at your phone use, so try to go through your morning routine and commute without using it. Enjoy your breakfast, read a newspaper, people watch on the train; wait until you're at your desk before you use your first screen.

Day 2: <u>Push Off</u>

Push notifications are essentially glorified interruptions and interjections in our day that we have sanctioned without even really thinking about it. It's time to rescind that permission: head into your settings and disable all of your push notifications so you're not seduced by those little red circles of temptation.

Day 3: <u>Unsubscribe, Unfollow, Unfriend</u>

It's a daunting task, but it's time to cull those burgeoning lists down to their most minimal, cleanest forms. Log in to your email and confront the mess. Instead of just sending them straight to junk, actually open them up and unsubscribe to stop them cluttering up your inbox again. Similarly, clean out your social media friends and follows, too. How many of those people and accounts do you really know, or talk to? Do you really need to know that your coworker's sister you met at that barbecue once is having pizza tonight?

Day 4: The Great Outdoors

Unfortunately, this is entirely weather-dependent, but the goal for the day is to get outside. Instead of looking at what you can remove from your day, this is more focused on adding valuable time and appreciating what you can do without being chained to a screen. The degree of your outdoor activity depends entirely on what you're comfortable with: go for a run after work, have some dinner al fresco, or if you can only sacrifice your lunchbreak, then go for a walk and find somewhere new to eat.

Day 5: Be Anti-Social

Facebook, Instagram, Twitter, Snapchat... any form of social media is off-limits today, both via phone and computer. Take the time this morning to log out of your accounts and disable your push notifications so you're not tempted to peek. Try connecting and being social with those physically around you instead.

Day 6: Off-Grid

Today is the day to completely disconnect; no phone, no computer, no screens. Try to spend the whole day independent of tech. Obviously it's easier if this day falls on a weekend, so feel free to rearrange your plan to accommodate this one.

Day 7: Setup

Use this day to shape your tech behavior over the next week. Stick a little post-it on the back of your phone with a message to remind you to take it easy when you next pick it up. Alternatively, take it a step further and try an app like *UnPlug* or *Moment* to set yourself a daily limit for your phone usage in advance.

<u>What to do if it didn't work out:</u>

Seven days has a lot of room for error, so if this plan was too difficult to stick to, try making some of the whole adjustments:

- The leap from two days to seven may have been too much; consider giving yourself a 'cheat day' in the middle and cut out Day 4 or 5.

- Instead of going completely off-grid on Day 6, try only allowing yourself tech-use during the first few hours of the morning and last few hours of the night.

- wIf it was the social media blackout on day that broke you, change it up so you're allowed to check your profiles, but only after dinner time. No, not during dinner; wait until you've finished eating, and then you can see what you've missed during the day.

▷ One Month

The 30-day plan is the longest of the plans and the toughest challenge. Whilst the weekend and 7-day plans are more focused on unplugging and resetting, this plan is built around developing healthier digital habits and a less tech-dependent lifestyle beyond the plan's 30-day structure.

Of course, as the longest plan, it has the most room for customization and adjustments. You should be coming to this having successfully gotten through the shorter plans, so take what you learnt about your own capabilities and behavior from those and apply them to this before you start. You know what works best for you, so plan and tweak in advance to ensure the best chance of success.

Goal:

Gradually decrease technology dependence over a period of thirty days, and start to introduce new tech-healthy habits to keep up beyond the detox.

Prep:

Like the one-week plan, the 30-day digital detox doesn't require that much prep, as the majority of changes will be made within the actual plan. Since this is a longer commitment, purchasing an alarm clock is recommended, as is purchasing some sort of notebook/journal to track your progress.

The Plan

Day 1: <u>Keep a Log</u>

Before you start, it's a good idea to assess the current state of things to assess your progress later. On your first day, monitor how long you're spending in front of a screen, and how many times you're picking up your phone. If it's too much to manually note, then download an app to do the number work for you.

Day 2: <u>Choose a Book</u>

You're going to have a lot more down time so choose a book and aim to finish it over the process. It gives you something to pick up when you're feeling twitchy and puts a nice cap of achievement for the month when you turn that last page.

Day 3: <u>Journal</u>

Whether you're writing out your day, jotting down notes, or even just planning or scheduling, journaling is a great analogue practice to pick up.

Day 4: <u>Get a Calendar</u>

Instead of relying on your computer or mobile calendar, invest in a planner or a desk calendar for work.

Day 5: <u>Designate No-Phone Zones</u>

Decide what areas of your home will be phone-free zones. The easiest one to start with? The bathroom. From there, designate at your discretion: it can be your whole bedroom or even just your bed.

Day 6: <u>Morning Routine</u>

Develop a tech-lite morning routine in which you don't look at any screens for the first hour of the day. This routine will be your go-to from here out.

Day 7: <u>Night Routine</u>

Plan out a routine at night that means you aren't looking at any screens for at least one hour before you go to sleep. If this means browsing etc. before that sixty minutes, so be it.

Day 8: <u>Tackle Your Inbox</u>

The email inbox… an overgrown wasteland filled with notification emails, newsletters and sale alerts from a forgotten age. It's time to do some pruning and clean it out. Mass delete emails, unsubscribe from unwanted alerts and flag addresses to go straight to junk in the future.

Day 9: <u>Cull Social Media</u>

Open any account that implements a friends list and trim it down. If you haven't spoke for a while and they're not an obligatory family add (we all have them), consider deleting them so your feed is only people you interact with and know on a personal level.

Day 10: <u>Delete Apps</u>

The last step in your tech-cull is to delete any distracting apps from your devices for the next month. What you keep and what you drop is up to you, but think carefully about the social media you keep, and the push notifications.

Day 11: Find a New Exercise

Get active by trying a new form of exercise out for the month. It could be anything from taking a dance class to going for a speed walk; any new activity keeps you busy and away from a screen.

Day 12: Limit Yourself to 5 Phone Checks

Exercise some self-discipline and only allow yourself to pick up and use your phone five times. This should keep you aware of your phone usage throughout the day.

Day 13: Embrace Grayscale

A former design ethicist at Google recommended switching your phone to grayscale to make it less tempting to pick up and less addictive to stay on.[1]

Day 14: No Out of Office Emails

From this point onwards, set your boundaries and minimize reading or replying to any work-related emails outside of office hours.

Day 15: Try a Disposable Camera

Instead of relying on your phone to take photos, buy a disposable camera to capture your day. You won't even have to run your shots through all those apps to get that old-school filter-feel.

Day 16: No Phone (3 Hours)

Set aside (a consecutive) three hours in which your phone remains firmly away from your grip. You might want to use a lock-out app to force your hand if need be.

Day 17: No Social Phone Use

Whenever you're in the company of others, your phone is strictly off-limits. Drinks with friends? No phone. Making a transaction at the store? No phone. The only conversations you can have today are face-to-face.

Day 18: No Solo Phone Use

Remember when you were a kid, and you used to have to make your own fun if you were bored? The same rule applies today. Whenever you find yourself alone, resist the urge to take your phone out. Pick up a book, start a puzzle, go for a walk: just no phones during alone time.

Day 19: No Phone Meals

Try eating all of your day's meals without looking at a screen. That means no picking up your phone, no browsing YouTube, no watching TV – just savor the meal.

Day 20: No Phone (6 Hours)

This is just an extended version of the Day 16 three-hour phone-ban; this time, choose a consecutive six hours to spend without your phone.

Day 21: Write a Letter

There's still something quite special about receiving a handwritten message from someone in the mail, so pick up a pen and write out a letter to a friend or family member.

Day 22: Phone-Free Journeys

Don't use your phone on any form of traverse: walking, in the car, commuting... if there's movement involved, keep that phone in your pocket.

Day 23: Use a Cookbook

Instead of falling into the endless-scrolling trap of looking for a recipe online, pick one out from a cookbook (or even a written recommendation from a friend or family member) and try out a new dish.

Day 24: Do Nothing

Take 15 minutes out to not do anything at all; just sit, take in the space around you, take a deep breath and allow your brain to turn off for a while.

Day 25: Leave Your Phone at Home

Make the conscious decision to leave you phone at home in the morning and go throughout your day without it.

Day 26: 30-Minute Wander

Set aside 30 minutes to just go for a wander. Take in your surroundings and take the time to reflect on your progress so far.

Day 27: <u>Let Your Phone Hit Zero</u>

Go through your day as usual... the only difference? No phone charger. Let your phone hit zero percent and don't recharge for the last two days of the month.

Day 28: <u>Go Outside</u>

Make a conscious effort to spend some time outdoors in some shape or form. Take your dog for a walk. Don't have a dog? Borrow one. Or go solo. Have a picnic. As long as there are no walls or roofs involved, your activity of choice qualifies.

Day 29: <u>Pick Five for Keepsies</u>

It's time to choose five day-tasks from the plan you want to repeat and keep up for the next month. The choice is entirely yours: go for the five you enjoyed most, or maybe pepper in a few that you found the most challenging and want to really conquer. Whatever you pick, keeping five tech-lite tasks will help encourage healthy digital habits as you transition out of the detox plan and back into your more regular routine.

Day 30: <u>Log and Compare</u>

It's time to log some new numbers and compare them with your Day 1 stats. See how much less you are picking up your phone (hopefully) than you were when you first started. Log your progress. If you're happy with that number, congratulations. If not, why not try to beat it in a month or two?

NOTES

Introduction

1. Culkin, J. (1967, March 18). A schoolman's guide to Marshall McLuhan. *Saturday Review*, 51–53: 70–72

Chapter 1: Diagnosis

What is Technology Addiction?

1. Alter, A. (2017). *Irresistible: The Rise of Addictive Technology and the Business of Keeping Us Hooked*

2. Gray, R. (2011, January 2). Facebook generation suffer information withdrawal syndrome. *The Telegraph* <https://www.telegraph.co.uk/technology/news/8235302/Facebook-generation-suffer-information-withdrawal-syndrome.html> (Accessed May 5, 2018)

The Toll of Technology

1. Digital Eye Strain. *The Vision Council* <https://www.thevisioncouncil.org/content/digdigi-eye-strain> (Accessed May 5, 2018)

2. Hansraj, K. K. (2014). Assessment of Stresses in the Cervical Spine Caused by Posture and Position of the Head. *Surgical Technology International, XXV:* 277-279

3. Shargorodsky J., Curhan S.G., Curhan G.C., Eavey R. (2010, August). Change in Prevalence of Hearing Loss in US Adolescents. *JAMA* 304(7):772–778

4. Mobile phones negatively affect male fertility, new study sug-

gests. *The University of Exeter* <http://www.exeter.ac.uk/news/featurednews/title_385859_en.html> (Accessed May 5, 2018)

5. Marder, B., Joinson, A. & Shankar, A. (2011). Saving Face on Facebook, An Investigation into Social Anxiety arising from presenting to Multiple Audiences within Social Network Sites. *Psychology Postgraduate Affairs Group Annual Conference.*

6. Tandoc, E., Ferrucci, P., Duffy, M. (2015, February). Facebook use, envy, and depression among college students: Is Facebooking depressing? *Computers in Human Behavior 43:* 139-146

Chapter 2: How to Start

Baby Steps

Starting Your Day Right

1. Global Mobile Consumer Survey. *Deloitte* <https://www2.deloitte.com/us/en/pages/technology-media-and-telecommunications/articles/global-mobile-consumer-survey-us-edition.html> (Accessed May 5, 2018)

2. Harris, T. (2016). How Technology Hijacks People's Minds—from a Magician and Google's Design Ethicist. <http://www.tristanharris.com/essays/> (Accessed May 5, 2018)

A Digitally Minimalist Home

1. Flacy, M., Nearly 1 in 5 people drop their smartphone in the toilet. *Digital Trends* <https://www.digitaltrends.com/mobile/nearly-1-in-5-people-drop-their-smartphone-in-the-toilet/> (Accessed May 5, 2018)

2. Verizon (2015). *True Wireless Confessions: How People Really Use Their Devices* <https://cbsdetroit.files.wordpress.com/2015/06/true-wireless-confessions-june-2015.pdf> (Accessed May 5, 2018)

Technology and Relationships

1. Przybylski, A.K., Weinstein, N. (2012). Can you connect with me now? How the presence of mobile communication technology influences face-to-face conversation quality. *Journal of Social and Personal Relationships* 30(3): 237-246

Chapter 3: How to Survive

Beating Procrastination and Staying Productive

1. McSpadden, K. (2015, May 14). You Now Have a Shorter Attention Span Than a Goldfish. *TIME Health* <http://time.com/3858309/attention-spans-goldfish/> (Accessed May 5, 2018)

Chapter 4: How to Thrive

The Importance of Doing Nothing

1. Fuller, T., (1732). *Gnomologia: adagies and proverbs; wise sentences and witty sayings, ancient and modern, foreign and British*

2. Schwartz, T. (2017), Relax! You'll Be More Productive. *The Energy Project* <https://theenergyproject.com/relax-youll-be-more-productive-2/> (Accessed May 5, 2018)

3. Confucius, *The Analects.*

4. Williams, R. (2014, August 15). Why reflection and 'doing nothing' are critical for productivity. *Financial Post* <http://business.financialpost.com/executive/leadership/why-reflection-and-doing-nothing-are-critical-for-productivity> (Accessed May 5, 2018)

5. Vincent, A. (2015, June 18). Yesterday: the song that started as Scrambled Eggs. *The Telegraph* <https://www.telegraph.co.uk/culture/music/the-beatles/11680415/Yesterday-the-song-that-started-as-Scrambled-Eggs.html> (Accessed May 5, 2018)